Standing on God's Promises
Not Sitting on His Premises

Michael Rucker
and
Pamela Rucker

PAGE PUBLISHING, INC.
New York, NY

First originally published by Page Publishing, Inc. 2019

ISBN 978-1-68456-128-5 (Hardcover)
ISBN 978-1-68456-127-8 (Digital)

Printed in the United States of America

Contents

Preface

THIS BOOK IS FOR THOSE who are in the body of Christ, who may be wondering why you are not experiencing a life of love, joy, peace, patience, kindness, goodness, faithfulness, gentleness, self-control, protection, rest, prosperity, positive critical thought, increased wisdom, and a deep aggressive desire to know God's purpose and will for your life. To experience these things, you must stand on the promises of God. What are God's promises? They are His declaration that He will do or refrain from doing something that will give life, love, joy, peace, patience, kindness, goodness, faithfulness, gentleness, self-control, protection, rest, prosperity, positive critical thought, increased wisdom, and a deep aggressive desire to know His purpose and will for your life, which you have a right to expect or claim the performance or forbearance of a specified act. If you are not experiencing these benefits of God's promises, you may be guilty of sitting on God's premises.

God promised Abram (Abraham) (1) a land; (2) to make him a great nation; (3) to bless him; (4) to make his name great; (5) to make him a blessing; (6) to bless those who bless him; (7) to curse those who cursed him; and (8) through him (Abraham), he would make his offspring numbered like the stars of the earth; (9) through Abraham's descendants, a child would be born, a son would be given, and the government would be on his shoulders[1]; (10) the increase of his government and peace would be no end. His name is Jesus, and He will be called Wonderful Counselor, Mighty God, Everlasting Father, Prince of Peace. He would reign on David's throne and over his kingdom, establishing and upholding it with justice and righteousness from that glory; no good thing will He withhold from those who walk upright.[2] God never promised us long life, but He promised us life beyond the grave. God's promises and blessings are guaranteed, but His blessings require cooperation on our part to walk in obedience to His Word.[3] We should not lose sight of the fact that all things work together for good to those who love God, to those who are called according to His purpose.

Acknowledgments

I, MICHAEL RUCKER, AM GRATEFUL for the relationship I had with my father, Roger Willis Rucker. Although he went to be with the Lord over thirty-two years ago, he was my template for being a man who protects and provides for his family. I dedicate this book to my dear mother, Dorothy J. Rucker, who went to be with the Lord on October 4, 2014. She worked tirelessly and made significant sacrifices for me and my siblings. She served as deaconess in our home church at Varick Memorial African Methodist Episcopal Zion Church in Northeast, Washington, DC, and traveled with me regularly to assist me during my tenure as pastor in Philadelphia, Pennsylvania. I thank God for her financial, moral, spiritual, and ministerial support with godly wisdom, which has molded me to be the man and minister I have become today.

Dorothy J. Rucker, February 2, 1930–October 4, 2014

To my dear sister and brother-in-law, Carolyn and Reginald Philson, and brother and sister-in-law, Roger and Doris Rucker, I give praises to God for them. I thank God for their godly example of marriage and the endless encouragement and love for me. I thank God for the example of perseverance my sister Rosalind Holton exhibited for the Rucker family throughout her marriage. I thank God for blessing me with twin daughters, LaTasha and Michelle Rucker; Tiffany Wilkins; and son, Charles Wilkins, and daughter-in-law, Adrienne Wilkins. Parenting sometimes brings diverse trials that will test your faith, but those trials have developed my perseverance to be mature and complete in my relationship with God. Parenting is the greatest leadership test of one's life.

Had it not been for the encouragement and mentoring from Dr. Lewis M. Anthony (now deceased), Dr. Gary W. Burns, Dr. Wilmer Frazier, all pastors of the African Methodist Episcopal Zion Church, Philadelphia–Baltimore Annual Conference, and Mid-Atlantic Episcopal District, I would not have been prepared to serve as senior pastor of Alleyne Memorial AME Zion Church in Philadelphia, Pennsylvania, from 1999 to 2002. Because of their love, care, and commitment to equip me, God used each of them in a powerful way to lay His foundation and purpose for my life in Christian ministry. Had it not been for the encouragement, nurturing, and spiritual mentoring from my aunt, Irma Johnson, I would not have pursued or accomplished my academic achievements.

I cannot forget my dearest friends Myron and Robin Aldridge. The encouragement and moral and financial support they provided was critical to the start of the church I planted in 2006, Truth Temple Bible Church. We have been close friends for more than twenty years. Except for Jesus Christ, I can't think of a better man to emulate than my friend and brother in the Lord, Myron Aldridge.

Finally, I thank God for my wife, Pamela, who I love as Christ loved the church and will give myself up for her to make her holy, cleansing her by washing her with water through God's Word to present her to myself as a radiant vessel without stain or wrinkle. I can't begin to express my appreciation of how she loves me, respects me, supports me, and encourages me. She is an incredible mother, wife, and woman of God. Without her I could not write this book or be the man God called me to be. It is with enormous gratitude and humility that God privileged me to have her as my wife.

*****

I, Pamela Rucker, am blessed to have been born by Herbert Lee Douglas and Lorraine Ellen Douglas. I, too, am grateful for the relationship I had with my father, Herbert Lee Douglas, who exchanged time for eternity in 2001. His thoughtfulness and support of others always permeated based on his military training. I thank God for his service in the United States Navy to our country. He was passionate about protecting the family unit and believed we are stronger together. I appreciate my mother, Lorraine Ellen Douglas, passionately known as Mom D, who was embraced by our entire community. Although she exchanged time for eternity in 2015, she leaves memories in history through her children. I am forever grateful for the unlimited opportunities, experiences, and infrastructure she established in the home to ensure we exceeded our expectation.

To my gifts from God, Charles and Tiffany, you are precious in my sight and my reason for being. I celebrate your differences, your love for God, how you both stretch our thinking territory to include today's perspective, your endless loving support, and determination to win. I also acknowledge my daughter-in-law, Adrienne Wilkins, who is a talented blessing and wonderful addition to our family.

To Sherman Douglas, my youngest brother, who presented me an example of pursuing his passion and surpassing his goal. His example of relentless determination and commitment affirmed that I, too, can follow my dreams and successfully reach my goals. To my oldest brother, Carl Crawford, who loves to share the Word of God; he never misses an opportunity to encourage me that I can do all things through Christ who strengthens us.

Much love to my circle of solid, positive influencers. You know who you are. Thank you for encouraging me and keeping me lifted in prayer.

Finally, to the love of my life, Michael L., my husband. I thank God for him daily. I celebrate his wisdom and life's journey. His wealth of knowledge and experience are indefatigable to see the bigger picture, and his willingness to help others is candidate for example and therefore worthy of emulation. The value he has added to my life is immeasurable. I love, honor, and respect him endlessly and thank him for making our home a place of sanctuary.

Introduction

State of Christianity and the Church

To BEGIN A DISCUSSION CONCERNING whether Christians are standing on the promises of God or sitting on the premises of God, we must examine the state of Christianity and the church, which will provide the critical points of focus. We must dig below the surface of what Christians believe and practice to determine your level of obedience to God's Word and commands. Below are results of research conducted by the Barna Group, which will provide some insight on what Christians believe and practice.

According to George Barna's research[4] for the American Culture and Faith Institute (ACFI), a national random sample of one thousand adults were asked about the morality of eight family-related behaviors. Large majorities of the public claimed that five of those behaviors are acceptable—either because they are morally acceptable or that they do not even qualify as moral issues (i.e., that choice is a matter of personal preference, and there is no right or wrong position related to the behavior). The five behaviors deemed acceptable by most US adults included the following: (1) using pills or medical devices for birth control—acceptable to 86 percent; (2) getting a divorce—acceptable to 77 percent; (3) sexual intercourse between unmarried male and female adults—acceptable to 71 percent; (4) having a baby without being married—acceptable to 69 percent; and (5) intentionally looking at pictures or videos that display nudity or explicit sexual behavior—acceptable to 58 percent. In addition, Barna reported about half of the nation (48 percent) said that having an abortion is acceptable. The only pair of family-related behaviors evaluated in the survey that smaller proportions of the public approved of were being married to more than one person at the same time (i.e., polygamy), which was endorsed by 28 percent; and physically or emotionally intimidating or aggressively dominating someone, deemed appropriate by 23 percent.

Barna also noted that at least 15 percent and as much as 40 percent of adults do not consider behaviors such as divorce, abortion, and unmarried sexual intercourse to be moral issues. In other words, there are no cultural or religious boundaries that dictate whether such behaviors are appropriate or inappropriate; those behaviors are simply a reflection of individual preferences. For the eight measures examined in the research, an average of one-quarter of all adults (25 percent) said those behaviors are not moral issues. One-third or more of the public considers divorce, birth control, and having a baby outside of marriage to be amoral decisions. These survey results and those listed below are alarming regarding moral views and behaviors. It's clear that believing in God and obedience to God's commands are lacking in the body of Christ, which will limit or even preclude them from receiving His promises and benefits of His blessings.

Ways in Which Faith Alignments Affect Moral Views
(percentage who say the behavior is either morally acceptable or it is not a moral issue)

| | --- Personal Faith-Group Affiliation--- | | | |
Moral Behavior	Christianity	Other Faith Group	Any Faith	Skeptics
using pills or medical devices for birth control	85%	84%	85%	90%
getting a divorce	72	81	73	91
sexual intercourse between unmarried adults	64	74	66	90
having a baby without getting married	63	66	64	87
intentionally looking at pictures or videos that display nudity or explicit sexual behavior	50	62	52	78
having an abortion	40	58	42	67
being married to more than one person at the same time	22	34	24	41
Intimidating or aggressively dominating someone	21	27	22	28

Source: American Culture & Faith Institute, FullView 18-4,
N=1000 U.S. adults, conducted March 2018

Barna further reported that many of the religious trends in America over the past decade or so are disheartening to Christians. Church attendance is down. Professions of faith are at low levels compared to the past, resulting in a declining percentage of born-again Christians. The number of people who label themselves as Christian is falling. Participation in small groups has dropped by half in less than a decade. The same pattern has characterized adult Sunday school involvement. Bible reading is less common. Even the number of adults who pray to God has decreased significantly in recent years. The question is why. While there is neither an easy explanation nor a single answer to that question, new research from the American Culture and Faith Institute (ACFI)[5] supplies one likely reason: Christians are not excited enough about their faith in and relationship with Jesus Christ to share the basics of that faith with nonbelievers. And that includes many Bible-believing pastors as well.

In a nationwide survey of adults, the ACFI study discovered that only two out of every ten adults (20 percent) believe they have a personal responsibility to share their faith in Christ with others who believe differently. While the numbers were higher for Christian-related subgroups of the population, those figures were not strikingly different. For instance, just 25 percent of those who call themselves Christian believe they are called to promote the gospel, a perspective shared by 31 percent of Protestants and 17 percent of Catholics. Even a minority of born-again Christians feel a sense of responsibility to share with others what they have personally experienced. There were surprisingly few differences across demographic segments of the population related to a sense of responsibility to evangelize. Unexpectedly, age made little difference in people's perspectives on their personal obligation to evangelize. In fact, there was no generation for which even one out of four people claimed to have such a responsibility. Hispanics and blacks were slightly more likely than whites to claim a responsibility to share their faith (25 percent versus 18 percent, respectively). There was no difference in the views of men and women on this matter.

ACFI also completed a parallel survey among a national sample of theologically conservative Protestant pastors. That study revealed that more than one out of every four of them (27 percent) do not believe they have a personal responsibility to share their faith in Christ with others who believe differently. Although there were no significant differences by age or race, the survey found that female pastors who are theologically conservative were substantially less likely than their male counterparts to claim a personal responsibility to evangelize (54 percent compared to 74 percent). Also, conservative pastors who had graduated from seminary were less likely to express an obligation to personally proclaim the gospel than were those who did not graduate from seminary. Denominationally, the survey found that conservative pastors associated with Baptist churches were the most likely to say they have a personal responsibility to evangelize (90 percent). That was considerably higher than among the theologically conservative pastors associated with Pentecostal (69 percent) or Holiness (76 percent) churches.

Unfortunately, the research found a high degree of consistency between people's lack of a sense of responsibility and their engagement in evangelism. Among adults, only 23 percent shared their personal faith on a monthly basis during the past year, and many of those who did share their faith either were not Christians or were sharing a version of Christianity that is not biblically grounded. In total, ACFI estimates that less than one out of every ten adults who shared a message about their faith with other people at least once a month during the previous year communicated a biblically accurate version of the gospel. As might be expected, theologically conservative Protestant pastors were more prone to actually sharing the gospel: 71 percent of them did so at least once a month during the past year.

The survey results among adults suggested that all kinds of divergent ideas about the Christian narrative are conveyed by people to nonbelievers. Among the concepts most likely to be shared by conservative believers are that people are basically good; that having some faith is more important than the substance of that faith; that God exists and is omnipotent and omniscient but that humankind has evolved from other life forms; He remains aware of what happens in the universe and is involved in our lives; there is absolute moral truth but it is located in various places; eternal security can be assured either through the sacrificial death and resurrection of Christ or by doing enough good deeds to earn God's favor; a person's life can be considered successful based upon the personal goals accomplished; the Bible is the reliable Word of God; Jesus understands our struggle because He sinned while on earth; and that sin is real but Satan and the Holy Spirit are not. The survey revealed that the more theologically liberal people are, the more likely they are to combine multiple unbiblical concepts into their presentation of the Christian faith.

Serious Problems for the Future

"The above findings raise an immediate and urgent challenge for the Christian Church in the US. A large majority of non-Christians in the US do not hear the gospel during a typical year. Worse, when they do have the Christian faith verbally presented to them, shockingly few hear a biblical form of the gospel," commented George Barna, who directed the research for ACFI. "Because of this, it is inevitable that the most common metrics of church life and personal spiritual maturity reflect rapid declines. When the fundamental message of Christianity is rarely communicated and then it is distorted in those infrequent situations when it is communicated, the outcome is not likely to be positive. This is one of the many unfortunate results of a nation in which only 10 percent of the public has a biblical worldview. You cannot give away what you do not possess, and clearly most Americans do not possess even a basic understanding of the Christian narrative as well as the purpose and implications of Jesus Christ's death and resurrection.

"Perhaps there are some hopeful signs found in the data from the clergy. Although it is troubling that more than one-quarter of them reject any personal responsibility to evangelize and three out of ten of them don't bother to share the gospel in a typical month, that leaves a majority of theologically conservative pastors ready and able to proclaim the gospel," Barna continued. "We know that close to nine out of ten of those pastors have a biblical worldview, so they are prepared to give a reason for the hope that is within them because of Jesus Christ. Although they are outnumbered by theologically moderate and liberal pastors, their numbers are substantial. Barna estimates there are seventy thousand churches in the US with biblically solid, evangelistic pastors. A concentrated effort by those pastors that boldly, clearly, and consistently proclaiming the gospel could certainly be the basis of a spiritual rebound in America." The surveys described are part of the Worldview Measurement Project conducted by ACFI to assess the state of America's worldview. The current studies are the first to be completed in that project and will serve as a benchmark for comparison in future years. The research described in this report is from two surveys conducted in February 2017. One of those surveys is FullView, a monthly national public opinion study conducted by the ACFI among a nationwide random sample of adults. This FullView online survey was conducted on February 1–5, 2017, with one thousand respondents aged eighteen or older, whose demographic profile reflects that of the United States. The second survey is the Conservative Clergy Canvass, known as ACFI's C3 survey, a national public opinion study conducted by ACFI among a sample of five hundred clergy who are part of ACFI's longitudinal panel of theologically conservative pastors. The C3 survey was conducted online during February 2017.

Chapter 1

Sitting on God's Premises

God's Premises

GOD'S PREMISES, AS DISCUSSED IN this book, refers to your statements about your practice and profession of faith as a proposition, principle, or assumption to prove your obligation of obedience and personal commitment to trust in God's Word, obey His commands, and endeavor to live a righteous life. To that end, sitting on God's premises points to your lack of discipleship (i.e., failure to go and make disciples of Jesus Christ teaching them all His commandments). Many presuppose that all people who go to church regularly are Christians; all Christians profess faith in Jesus Christ as Savior; and therefore, all Christians trust in God's Word, obey His commands, and sincerely endeavor to live a righteous life. That presupposition is far from the truth. If you subscribe to this presupposition, you may be sitting on God's premises instead of standing on His promises. If you don't seek first the kingdom (i.e., reign, rule, or authority) of God and His righteousness, all the things you need and desire will not be added to you. Simply put, if you receive and believe but don't become a disciple of Christ, you are sitting on the premises of God.

What it Means to Sit on God's Premises

Your horizontal relationship with people will mirror your vertical relationship with the Almighty. According to survey results reported by George Barna concerning the state of the Christian Church and how Americans express their faith, "Americans express their faith in a variety of ways. While regular church attendance is a reliable indicator of faithful Christian practice, many Americans choose to experience and express their faith in a variety of other ways, the most common of which is prayer. For instance, three-quarters of Americans (75 percent) claim to have prayed to God in the last week. This represents 73 percent who self-identify as Christian. Following prayer, the next most common activity related to faith practice is attending a church service, with more than one-third of adults (35 percent) having sat in a pew in the last seven days, not including a special event such as a wedding or funeral. About the same proportion (34 percent) claim to have read the Bible on their own, not including when they were at a church or synagogue. About one in six American adults have either volunteered at a nonprofit (19 percent) or at church (18 percent) in the last week. Slightly fewer attended Sunday school (17 percent) or a small group (16 percent)."

What these results fail to show is the horizontal relationship with people. These results fail to show how accountable Christians are with obeying God's commands in their personal, professional, and social interactions with others. It's obedience to God's commands that determine whether Christians experience a life of love, joy, peace, patience, kindness, goodness, faithfulness, gentleness, self-control, protection, rest, prosperity, positive critical thought, increased wisdom, and a deep aggressive desire to know His purpose and will for their life. However, the results do show the religious makeup of the United States and what they believe. Barna uses seven key faith groups in America: (1) born-again Christians, (2) evangelical Christians, (3) those who are Bible-minded, (4) churched/unchurched, (5) practicing Christian, (6) nonpracticing Christian, and (7) post-Christian. He defines **born-again Christians** as those who have made a personal commitment to Jesus Christ that is still important in their life today and believe that, when they die, they will go to heaven because they have confessed their sins and accepted Jesus Christ as their savior. **Evangelical Christians** are those who meet the born-again criteria plus seven other conditions. The seven conditions include saying their faith is very important in their life today; believing they have a personal responsibility to share their religious beliefs about Christ with non-Christians; believing that Satan exists; believing that Jesus Christ lived a sinless life on earth; asserting that the Bible is accurate in all that it teaches; believing that eternal salvation is possible only through grace, not works; and describing God as the all-knowing, all-powerful, perfect deity who created the universe and still rules it today. Being classified as an evangelical is not dependent upon church attendance or the denominational affiliation of the church attended. **Bible-minded** are those who believe the Bible is accurate in all the principles it teaches and have read the scriptures within the past week. **Churched/unchurched** are those who attended church in the past month or those who have not attended church in the past six months. **Practicing Christians** are those who attend a religious service at least once a month and who say their faith is very important in their lives and self-identify as a Christian. **Nonpracticing Christians** are those who self-identify as a Christian but do not qualify as a practicing Christian. **Post-Christian** are those who do not believe in God or identify as atheist or agnostic, and they do not participate in practices such as Bible reading, prayer, and church attendance. Based on this metric, almost half of all American adults (48 percent) are post-Christian (meet 60 percent or more, or nine or more, of the following factors below). Highly post-Christian individuals meet 80 percent or more of the factors below (12 or more of these 15 criteria):

1. Do not believe in God
2. Identify as atheist or agnostic
3. Disagree that faith is important in their lives
4. Have not prayed to God (in the last year)
5. Have never made a commitment to Jesus
6. Disagree the Bible is accurate
7. Have not donated money to a church (in the last year)
8. Have not attended a Christian church (in the last year)
9. Agree that Jesus committed sins
10. Do not feel a responsibility to share their faith
11. Have not read the Bible (in the last week)
12. Have not volunteered at church (in the last week)
13. Have not attended Sunday school (in the last week)
14. Have not attended religious small group (in the last week)
15. Do not participate in a house church (in the last year)

According to these key faith identifiers, three are critical. Born-again Christians make up one-third of the population (35 percent). They are defined as those who made a personal commitment to Jesus

Christ that is still important in their life today and believe that, when they die, they will go to heaven because they have confessed their sins and accepted Jesus Christ as their savior; **but not Lord.** This suggests a lack of obedience to God's commands and principles. The next largest group was those considered Bible-minded, who make up about one-quarter of the population (23 percent). They believe the Bible is accurate in all the principles it teaches and have read the scriptures within the past week, **but no reception of Jesus Christ as Lord and Savior.** Another key factor, according to Barna's research, is a surprising proportion of **churchgoing Christians in the US are generally unaware of the Great Commission** ("Research Releases in Faith and Christianity," March 27, 2018). When asked if they had previously heard of the Great Commission, half of US churchgoers (51 percent) say they do not know this term. Finally, the next significant group, post-Christians made up almost half of the American adult population (48 percent). They **do not believe in God or identify as atheist or agnostic, and they do not participate in practices such as Bible reading, prayer, and church attendance.** These three factors are critical with regard to whether Americans are standing on the promises of God. In fact, it represents Americans who sit on the premises of God.

What Christians practice and believe significantly impacts their obedience to Christ and His commands and their ability to be and make disciples. For example, Christ's Sermon on the Mount[6] describes what Christian's attitudes and actions should be (e.g., those who are poor in spirit, those who mourn, those who are meek, those who hunger and thirst for righteousness, those who are merciful, those who are pure in heart, those who are peacemakers, those who are persecuted because of righteousness, and those who are insulted and falsely accused of all kinds of evil because of Christ) and the blessings that come from exhibiting those attitudes and actions. It also describes social or human behaviors that Christians must not exhibit in obedience to Christ (e.g., murder, adultery, fornication, divorce, revenge, etc.). The Sermon on the Mount further teaches the thoughts of man and what is in his heart concerning the identified behaviors can result in one sinning against God and man.

Christian Life When Sitting on God's Premises

Don't miss the promises of God for your life by sitting on the premises, allowing secular worldviews and other's beliefs and opinions to block your blessings. Sitting on God's premises is when you fail to go and make disciples; fail to believe in the authority of scripture; fail to exhibit a life of love, joy, peace, patience, kindness, goodness, faithfulness, gentleness, self-control, protection, rest, and prosperity; and fail to exhibit positive critical thought, increased wisdom, and a deep aggressive desire to know God's purpose and will for your life. Most of us get stuck sitting on God's premises because we keep practicing the same spiritual behaviors and expect different results. We don't forgive, pray without ceasing, or address our anger before the sun sets. Spiritual behaviors are a crucial part of spiritual growth, but when the same spiritual behaviors become routine, they need to be changed. What got you where you are spiritually may not get you where God wants you to go next. With the inauguration of President Trump, followed by record-setting Women's Marches; Hurricanes Irma, Harvey, Jose, and Maria battering the Caribbean and the southern United States; Americans witnessed natural disasters; a slew of sexual misconduct allegations launching the #MeToo movement; tragic violence in Las Vegas, New York, Charlottesville, Parkland, Sutherland, and Santa Fe shook the country; and confirmation of Judge Brett Kavanagh to the Supreme Court. In times like these Christian life can be reduced to sitting on God's premises.

An example of what it looks like to sit on the premises of God is when Christians claim to be spiritual but not religious[7] or love Jesus but not the church.[8] Those who claim to be spiritual but not religious hold unorthodox views about God, are ambivalent toward religion, and take part in more informal and individual modes of spiritual practice. They do not claim any faith at all. They say they are spiritual, but they identify as either atheist, agnostic, or unaffiliated with a specific religion. Being spiritual but not religious suggests that you fail to agree with the institution of the church or refuse to submit to the authority of the church leadership or church polity. You hold tightly to Christian belief; you just do not find value in the church as a component of that belief. If you fall within this group, you are sitting on God's premises. Regarding those who love Jesus but not the church, they self-identify as Christian and strongly agree that their religious faith is very important in their life but are *de-churched* (have attended church in the past but haven't done so in the last six months or more). They strongly identify with their faith (they say their religious faith is very important in their life today). They just don't attend church. This group still holds very orthodox Christian views of God and maintains many of the Christian practices (albeit individual ones over corporate ones). Loving God but not the church suggests that you have primarily rejected religion and prefer instead to define your own boundaries for spirituality—often mixing beliefs and practices from a variety of religions and traditions. You live out your spirituality in the absence of the institutional church but still take part in a set of spiritual practices, albeit a mishmash of them. Somewhat unsurprisingly, those who love God but not the church are *very* unlikely to take part in the most *religious* practices like scripture reading, prayer, and even groups or retreats, particularly compared to the other religious groups. Their spiritual nourishment is found in more informal practices like yoga, meditation, and silence or solitude. Their most common spiritual practice is spending time in nature for reflection. If you love God but not the church, you are sitting on the premises of God.

Another example of what it looks like to sit on the premises of God is when you seek the wisdom of talk show hosts when asked questions such as "What must one do to initiate sex with their significant other?" It raises questions of whether the question is being asked of heterosexual and homosexual married couples and singles. Based on Barna's survey article, as much as 40 percent of adults do not consider behaviors such as unmarried sexual intercourse to be a moral issue (i.e., a sin). This question was asked on the talk show *The Real*, an Emmy Award–winning daytime talk show on Fox 5. While only one of the talk show hosts, who is heterosexual and married, answered the question, millions of Americans who viewed that broadcast may likely apply this subject of discussion to both heterosexual and homosexual single and married couples. Those who are single and profess to be Christian may believe it's okay to engage in sex with your significant other before marriage. Those who profess to be Christian may believe it's okay to engage in sexual activity prior to marriage. The hosts of *The Real* made no distinction or clarification to determine whether significant other meant a spouse or someone you were dating or whether you were heterosexual or homosexual. When presented this way, the American public and practicing Christians could likely perceive this as relative for everyone: heterosexual and homosexual married or single. Note, this is not an affirmation that practicing or professing Christians who are homosexual and married to a same-sex partner are acceptable lifestyles or behaviors that God would approve.

Another example is when talk show host Wendy Williams made a statement that she would not trust a man who did not drink, did not have a smoke, or not had sex. Ms. Williams made this statement in response to an individual in the audience who wanted to know if she should trust her boyfriend. While she didn't explain the basis of her statement, it could lead one to believe that it's better to trust a boyfriend who is experienced, who drinks, who smokes, and who is not a virgin. She never mentioned a concern about whether the boyfriend had faith in God. We sit on the premises of God when we allow other's beliefs and what media and the world deems relative and not make specific distinctions of what media and the world says versus what God allows and prohibits in scripture. When we don't identify sin as scripture does, we are sitting on the premises of God. When we don't search scripture to answer questions concerning social and moral behavior, we sit on the premises of God. My point is the world says it's okay to have sex before marriage and calls homosexuality and same-sex marriage an alternative lifestyle, which doesn't offend those who indulge in it, but turns a blind eye that encourages tolerance of such behaviors which are inconsistent with God's Word.

In Barna's article on competing worldviews that influence today's Christians (Barna "Research Releases in Culture and Media," May 9, 2017), 31 percent of practicing Christians agree that "all people pray to the same god or spirit, no matter what name they use for that spiritual being." They also have the belief that "meaning and purpose come from becoming one with all that is." Barna also found 32 percent of practicing Christians strongly agree that "if you do good, you will receive good; and if you do bad, you will receive bad." He said this karmic statement, though not explicitly from scripture, appeals to many Christians' sense of ultimate justice. Twenty-three percent of practicing Christians strongly agree that "what is morally right or wrong depends on what an individual believes." Another Barna study found that 52 percent of practicing Christians strongly agree that the Bible teaches that "God helps those who help themselves." Sixty-one percent of practicing Christians embrace at least one of these ideas. We sit on God's premises when we focus on all the distractions of the world, e.g., nonproductive relationships that add no value to you and block your growth opportunities and unhealthy relationships or social circles that add sorrow, drain you, and are toxic. Examples of these are the deceptive behaviors and social maliciousness women exhibit on television shows such as *Housewives of Atlanta* and *Housewives of Potomac*. Christians who feed their spirit with such reality shows run the risk of adversely affecting their moral compass, witness, and their walk, thereby positioning them to sit on God's premises instead of standing on God's promises. Other distractions are the breaking news from the news media and programming, which in most cases result in emotional distractions of the public; invalid or misinformation; and alarming fads, patterns, and trends that could result in the death of your faith, finances, and family relationships. Excepting opportunities that are not within the scope of God's purpose for your life or submitting to someone else's ad hoc role for you can result in you sitting on the premises of God. Because someone else may succeed doing or being something other than what you do or become does not mean you would succeed at what they do or become.

God's people must know distractions from the world are designed to cause you to lose and not be victorious and distort your biblical worldview. This is a sign you are sitting on God's premises. Other signs of sitting on God's premises include but are not limited to chasing after social media instead of chasing after God; no pursuit of God's plan for your life; and when one does not intentionally or purposely give God first place in their life. God should not be an option; He should be a priority. Each day should start with Him at the forefront. Sitting on God's premises also include allowing others who don't stand on God's promises to dictate your future, such as those in positions of celebrity status, leadership, and power who routinely exhibit unrighteous thoughts, words, and deeds. Other signs of sitting on God's premises are the lack of knowledge about God's promises and benefits when not standing on them; not spending enough time in the presence of God through prayer and study of His Word; no growth in your life[9] spirituality, physically, mentally, personally, professionally, financially, and socially. An example of this is that as an employee, we are responsible for knowing our job or craft, working as unto God, rendering unto Caesar[10] what's Caesar's, and rendering unto God what's God's. If we have implemented this as our standard practice, there is no reason you should allow negative influences to kill your spirit as a professional. The enemy comes to steal, kill, and destroy. In addition, within family and social circles, if you have done your due diligence to serve the Lord and are living the righteous life you desire, do not allow negative forces to destroy your joy[11] of the Lord.

God uniquely made all of us with skills and talents to make a difference in the earth.[12] We're not walking in our purpose nor making an impact in the earth when we do not use our gifts. God created us with a brain to store information and use it when needed, yet we allow other's authority to derail our blessing. The brain is arguably the most important organ in the human body. It controls and coordinates actions and reactions, allows us to think and feel, and enables us to have memories and feelings—all the things that make us human. Our brain is an important tool God wants us to use. When we use our brain and His Word to guide how we think, we can accomplish a lot to further the kingdom of God. We are responsible for our future, opportunities, and growth. You may have heard it said, "Get with those who have your answer." What does this mean? Does this mean we should seek those who appear to be or are going in the direction we believe God desires for us? If God is our answer and we keep learning His way of doing business and living, we will reach our expected end that He desires for us. This certainly can minimize making man our god, serving or fulfilling his desires, and never accomplishing God's purpose for us and our family. If God is not our answer we are sitting on His premises and will not reach our expected end.

God has a calling on our lives to serve Him using the gifts He gives us. The Bible tells us that the one who serves is the one who will be great in the kingdom of God.[13] From the time we are saved (i.e., receive Jesus Christ as our Savior and Lord), we are commanded to serve Him until the day we physically die. Therefore, we should ask ourselves daily if we are doing what God called us to do. If we are not, we are sitting on the premises of God. This reminds me of an illustration by Dr. Tony Evans, senior pastor of Oak Cliff Bible Fellowship in Dallas, Texas, which I have modified. To summarize it, he said when we purchase expensive items and they are defective, we must thank God for warrantees if we need to return the item for repair, replacement, or refund. Jesus Christ purchased us with his life which is His warrantee for us if we need repair, replacing, or refund. If we don't receive Christ as Lord and Savior, we cannot be repaired, which would leave us sitting on God's premises. If we don't die, we cannot be replaced with a life of service to Christ and would therefore be sitting on God's premises. If we don't make disciples, the kingdom of God has no refund as payment forward for our lives. When God's purpose for our lives are not met, we are sitting on God's premises.

When greed, consumerism, hate, secular humanism, and lack of biblical truth supersede love, we sit on the premises of God. I would like to note, America sits on the premises of God. America is practicing ungodliness as we kick God out of our schools and all aspects of our public life. America is practicing unrighteousness in the daily murder of babies (Roe v. Wade) and racism in the criminal justice system (see *The New Jim Crow: Mass Incarceration in the Age of Colorblindness* by Michelle Alexander and *The Black and the Blue* by Matthew Horace and Ron Harris). America suppresses the truth in exchange for what the world says is truth. Americans today live for themselves instead of the Savior. Americans today are worshiping the creation rather than the creator. America was built and made prosperous because it stood on the promises of God, but it currently sits on the premises of God in the worst way.

Standing on God's Promises

God's Promises

Those in the body of Christ must know and understand the Bible teaches and tells us of the promises God made to mankind through His call of Abraham.[14] In the Old Testament, He promised Abraham the following: (1) a land; (2) a great nation through his descendants; (3) a blessing that would affect all the nations of the earth; (4) to bless those who blessed him; and (5) to curse those who cursed him. God's promises to and blessings for Abraham extend not only to his physical descendants (i.e., believing Jews) but also to all, who in true faith embrace and follow Jesus Christ the true seed of Abraham.[15] All who possess faith like Abraham's are children of Abraham's[16] and are blessed along with him.[17] They become Abraham's offspring, heirs according to the promise,[18] which includes receiving by faith the promise of the Spirit in Christ Jesus. However, God's promises require an obligation of obedience and personal commitment to Him. Obedience and commitment to God entail trust in God's Word, obedience to His commands, and sincere endeavor to live a righteous life. Any profession of faith in Jesus Christ as Savior and Lord that does not involve obedience to Him as Lord is not true saving faith. If you have no true saving faith in Jesus Christ, you will not become a true disciple of Christ or receive or experience the benefits of God's promises and blessings.

In the New Testament, God, through faith in the death, burial, and resurrection of His Son, Jesus Christ, promised salvation and eternal life.[19] He presented Jesus as the Jewish Messiah sent by Him to fulfill Old Testament prophecy. He also promised us the benefits of being poor in spirit, mourning, being meek, hungering and thirsting for righteousness, being merciful, being pure in heart, being a peacemaker, and being persecuted for righteousness. Great is our reward in heaven when persecuted and falsely accused for Christ's sake.

What It Means to Stand on God's Promises

We must trust in our hearts that God will fight our battles and is faithful to fulfill all His promises to us according to His Word.[20] An example of this is when the Israelites were being pursued by the Pharaoh toward the Red Sea. They were terrified and cried out to God. They asked Moses why he brought them to the desert to die. Moses told them not to be afraid and to stand firm and see the deliverance the Lord would bring them that day. Moses believed in his heart that God would fight their battle and deliver them from the Pharaoh. When we face various battles in our lives, we must believe God will fight for us and expect a victorious outcome. We must know and believe our strength comes from God. The Bible tells us we can receive strength from the Lord[21] and can rest knowing God has compassion for us,[22] which means we do not have to walk in fear.[23] When tragedy strikes, we must stand on the promises of God. If we lack wisdom in areas of our lives, we can ask God for wisdom.[24] Additionally, it is important to have fellowship with faithful believers in Jesus Christ as Savior and Lord, so we can grow and be our brother's keeper. When we fall short of the glory of God and confess our sins to Him, He is faithful and just to forgive us and cleanse us from all unrighteousness.[25] Standing on God's promises means you believe that God is, you trust what God says, you obey His commands, and you apply His principles when making decisions in your life. You stand on the authority of scripture and not the authority of the world's view.

Christian Life When Standing on God's Promises

What is life like when you're standing on God's promises? Standing on God's promises is doing the right thing when no one is watching and providing an example of holy living before others. Standing on God's promises is when your lifestyle aligns with godly principles. Standing on God's promises allows you to receive favor when such favor appears unfair. For example, you are selected for a job even though you were not as qualified as other candidates considered. God qualifies those whom He calls. When standing on God's promises, you receive biblical insight and wisdom to become a go-to person to answer life's spiritual and moral questions others may have. Standing on God's promises is including God in all your conversations with others and making disciples and confessing Christ before men.[26] You may wonder why persons reach out to you for answers to their personal, moral, and spiritual dilemmas. When you stand on God's promises, you will desire to grow those around you so they become the best they can be to fulfill God's purpose in their lives. You may experience struggles in your family relationships, marriage relationships (if married), business relationships in your workplace, and in practicing and experiencing faith in the church. But if you stand on God's promises, He will take you through your struggles and you will experience the blessings and benefits of love, joy, peace, patience, kindness, goodness, faithfulness, gentleness, self-control, protection, rest, prosperity,[27] positive critical thought, increased wisdom, and identifying your purpose in life to leave a legacy in the earth.

With regard to increased wisdom, if you seek wisdom, you will understand the fear of the Lord. The fear of the Lord is the beginning of knowledge, and that knowledge will enable you to attain knowledge of God. God will give you wisdom. When you stand on God's promises, God will give you wisdom and provide a shield to the upright, guard the paths of justice, and preserve the way of His saints. When God puts wisdom in your heart, it becomes pleasant to your soul and discretion will preserve you; understanding will keep you and deliver you from evil.[28] This is the value of God's wisdom. When you stand on God's promises, you must pick up your cross and carry it as Christ did for us. Picking up your cross and carrying it may mean being abandoned by coworkers, family, and friends; standing alone on matters inconsistent with God's Word; and allowing God to change you when His wisdom reveals to you that you were wrong in your thoughts, words, and deeds. Standing on God's promises does not mean your life will be problem free, but it will be victorious.

America has deviated from standing on the promises of God. The moral decline in this country will result in its implosion from the inside and God's judgment. America's enemies will not have to fire one missile or nuclear warhead to destroy it because it's being destroyed from the inside out. Those who have an ear, let them hear what the Lord has to say; if you obey God's commands, He will set you high above all nations of the earth (Deuteronomy 28:1). America was set high above all nations but is being brought low because of its sin.

Chapter 2

Life's Journey Standing on God's Promises

M. Lamont Rucker

YOUR LIFE JOURNEY WILL ALWAYS include setbacks, setups, successes, failures, hurts, disappointments, and victories. Because all have sinned and fall short of the glory of God, it is imperative that believers stand on God's promises. I, Michael Rucker, have been privileged to receive exposure to life-changing experiences, achieve academically, and grow spiritually and professionally as a leader, which exceeded all my personal expectations. As I reflect on my life's journey, I realize that God's promises were at work on my behalf.

In my early years from puberty to adolescence, I always wanted to help others, particularly my mother. I was not a perfect child, but I always wanted people to like me and accept me. My mother always took me to church to attend Sunday school and Sunday worship service and insisted that I attend as I became a young adult. During the puberty and adolescence years, I never understood or heard from the pulpit that I could be saved and receive eternal life if I believed in Jesus Christ. I experienced what most teenagers and young adults experienced. Yes, I drank alcohol, used profanity at times, was interested in girls, but didn't date many girls because I was a little fat boy who girls just didn't want to associate with unless I looked like actor Denzel Washington. When I did date, my hormones were all over the place and I wanted to have sex just like the other male friends of mine. I did many of the mischievous things that young men my age did. However, I believe God's promises were active in my life then because of my mother and great-aunt's prayers.

During my senior high school years and early college years at Jackson State College in Jackson, Mississippi, I totally strayed from church and did not exhibit godly behavior. I was still considered a nice guy, but I was not following biblical principles. Nice guys don't get saved or receive eternal life if they don't receive the Lord Jesus Christ as their personal Savior and Lord. I played high school football and thought I was all that and a bag of chips. I was popular in high school and dated a young lady who I got pregnant but aborted the pregnancy. I asked God to forgive me and her. That relationship ended, but I carried the pain of it all for some time until I could forgive myself. I did other things I am not proud of as a young man, but time and time again, I found myself asking God to forgive me.

After returning from Jackson, Mississippi, I was privileged to serve in the federal government for four years as an environmental science intern, followed by twenty-six years as a human resource professional. I remember being interviewed for a senior level position with the Social Security Administration in Baltimore, Maryland. Toward the end of that interview, the interview panel asked me where I saw myself within the next five years. My response was "I see myself pastoring a church." At that moment, I wasn't sure where that came from, but I believe it was the Lord speaking. Shortly thereafter, I became more active in my church and served as Christian Education Director, licensed as a local preacher in the African Methodist Episcopal Zion church, and later ordained as an elder. God's promises were at work in my life. During my tenure in federal government service, I became a father of twin daughters, was married, and accepted my calling to the pastoral ministry. Subsequent to retiring as a federal employee, I served fifteen years as a contract consultant to the federal government in human resources management. At that time, with the help of the Holy Spirit and God's Word, I purposed in my heart to stand on God's promises. God utilized Rev. Dr. Gary Burns and Rev. Dr. Wilmer Frazier as my mentors in ministry to prepare me for pastoral ministry service. I served as an associate minister under their leadership for several years in the African Methodist Episcopal Zion (AMEZ) Church and later was appointed senior pastor to an AMEZ Church in Philadelphia, Pennsylvania. I later received a scholarship to attend seminary. I never imagined I would be able to go to seminary, but I believe God's promises were at work in my life on this matter. My seminary experience reaffirmed and confirmed God's plan for my life because I stood on His promises all the more. However, as with many of us, life crisis can derail our best efforts. I experienced several unfortunate challenges as a pastor, husband, and father. I became a grandfather and divorced my first wife. As a result, I thought God could no longer use me as a minister of the gospel. I also thought I failed as a husband, father, and pastor. It was difficult to stand on God's promises, but God, through His forgiveness, healing, favor, and grace, restored my confidence as a husband, as a father, and to continue in my calling.

After divorce, life took on a different meaning with changes. I clearly understand why God hates divorce. It took the grace of God, through his promises, to help and heal me. I stepped down from the pastoral ministry to heal. At which time, I joined the First Baptist Church of Glenarden (FBCG). I chose to not serve in any ministry as a leader or serve on the FBCG ministerial staff. Since that time, God has used the teaching and preaching of Pastor John K. Jenkins Sr. to encourage and heal my spirit. God later led me to the most wonderful woman who is right for me, who I am now married to. Through this marriage, I gained another daughter and a son. Presently, on a referral basis, I conduct marital counseling and prepare couples for engagement, building and assessing their relationships for marriage. In addition, my lovely wife and I created a foundation to help inner-city youth who are underserved. I await my next service assignment from God, the Holy Spirit. As I grow older, I am able to see God clearer. Thus, a note for us all: Our aging is God's tool which turns the pages of our lives and priorities so we can see Him clearer.

Pamela A. Rucker

I, Pamela Rucker, was raised in a Christian environment, and while things were not perfect, they were okay as far as I knew. Our community environment was very challenging due to the elements of most urban areas. For this reason, my mother enrolled me in activities outside of our immediate environment. She was an avid forward-leaning planner and researcher who intentionally ensured all bases were covered to meet the needs of her children. In addition, she purposely secured the tools, resources, and opportunities for us to be successful and grow. This infrastructure embedded the same practices within me. I was a product of my environment and its flaws until I refreshed the embedded behavior learned.

As a youngster, in middle and high school, I thoroughly enjoyed and participated in sports and extracurricular activities, which allowed travel opportunities across the District of Columbia metropolitan area. Sports activities were a way of escape and hope, which was a blessing in many ways. During this time, I received a need-based Foundation Award. Upon receipt of the award, I made a commitment to someday establish a foundation to meet the needs of the underserved in honor and recognition of what was done for me. Our foundation was established in 2013. Praise the Lord.

While attending high school, I met a powerful community leader. I never imagined our engagement would result in a life-long partnership of community services. John Francis "Peterbug" Matthews was a conduit to lay the foundation for the promises of God during my formative years. He was a pioneer and known pillar in the community, recognized as a well-connected frontiersman with access to resources to support community-based initiatives for future leaders. Mr. Matthews gave me specific instructions to follow that changed the course and trajectory of my life. Based on his recommendation, I attended the University of the District of Columbia and served as a youth advocate in support of community-based initiatives. For this I am grateful.

Early on in my federal government career, I met two solid civil servants, Lucille Blakley and Doretta Davis, who both served in positions of leadership. God used them in my life as vessels who added personal and professional infrastructure, safety, and stability. Following their guidance allowed me to see the promises of God in my life. These ladies gave meaning to my understanding of Philippians 4:8 (NLT). "And now, dear brothers and sisters, one final thing. Fix your thoughts on what is true, and honorable, and right, and pure, and lovely, and admirable. Think about things that are excellent and worthy of praise." Fellowship in positive energy was priceless. This practice allowed me to experience the promises of God. Today, I work tirelessly to eliminate negative energy from my life.

The Lord Blessed me with two amazing children Charles E. Wilkins Jr. and Tiffany B. Wilkins. Upon receipt of my gifts from God, I committed to provide a safe and loving home. My assignment was to love them with every fiber of my being. I celebrate their differences, talents, accomplishments, and needs. I commit to love them with the love of the Lord and assist them through life's journey when needed. I am most proud to know they love the Lord. I look forward to seeing them raise their families in a loving and nurturing environment.

Throughout my life, I have served in ministry, completed ministry internship courses, and attended church since childhood. During my journey, God placed many wonderful people in my path. Some of whom have blessed me beyond measure. For this reason, I, too, enjoy supporting and assisting others in kind. I have also experienced not so kind calculated situations from unexpected individuals. While this was very painful, it was also an opportunity to grow. I have not arrived at a place of perfection; however, I am truly grateful to God for loving me, flaws and all. I am clear, while we fall short, we must continue to assess who we allow to have platforms in our lives. In doing so, we can protect ourselves from further harm. The most powerful experiences for me were the positive energy influencers who saw my potential and nurtured me in a positive direction toward a path for success. I believe information and opportunities are available; however, it's what we do individually with the information provided that allows us to stand on the promises of God and experience the results. As I look back, all my experiences were necessary, complete, and perfect.

Dr. and Mrs. Rucker

Dr. Rucker officiating his stepson's wedding.

Chapter 3

Conclusions, Observations, and Recommendations

ALTHOUGH WE LIVE IN A post-Christian society, God's promises are available to anyone and everyone who choose to accept Him as Savior and Lord and are obedient to His commands. Members of the body of Christ are personally responsible for knowing God for themselves and knowing what is in His Word. Christians must independently practice trusting what they have read in God's Word and implement godly lifestyles and principles to see the presence of God in their lives. It is a bad practice to solely know and trust God through someone else's life and guidance unless they live according to the commands of Christ; and how would one know this unless they know God's Word for themselves. Knowing your Lord and Savior is a personal journey with Him and enhanced by scripture, movement of the Holy Spirit, miracles, and other believers' testimonies.

Are Christians Losing Their Way?

The Barna Group attempted to make sense of American public opinion on a range of issues related to our daily lives and faith journeys. So he compiled the top ten most-read articles of 2017 from his website. While each of those articles are important, we believe article topics number two, "Competing Worldviews Influence Today's Christians"; number seven, "The Aging of America's Pastors"; number eight, "Tech Habits Changing the American Home"; and number ten, "Meet the 'Spiritual but Not Religious'" as critical to one's ability to receive the benefits of God's promises and blessings. We believe these four survey results impact the body of Christ's ability to be obedient to God's commands and to live a righteous life. We also believe Christians today are replacing the authority of scripture to human consensus, theologically and secularly. Consensus can lead one to worshipping other gods. The jury is still out on the Beyoncé Mass[29] held by Rev. Yolanda M. Norton, PhD candidate at Vanderbilt

University in Hebrew Bible and Ancient Israel and professor at San Francisco Theological Seminary. While I support women in ministry and encouraged by some of feminist theology, I pray feminist theology does not take the gospel of Jesus Christ beyond the bounds of biblical truth outlined in God's Word.

In America, according to Barna (*Barna Trends 2018*), the term *post-truth* is now used to describe the current political climate in which reality is relative and facts are open to interpretation. He reported that truth is increasingly being regarded as something felt or relative. He also reported that many Americans, particularly millennials, don't feel that any one religious text has a monopoly on truth but that they are all different expressions of the same spiritual message. Because of this, some spiritually inclined Americans seek faith outside of the local church context, as is the case with those who are *spiritual but not religious*[30] or those who *love Jesus but not the church*.[31] According to a Pew Research Center study,[32] a share of Americans who believe in God with absolute certainty has declined in recent years, while a share saying they have doubts about God's existence— or that they do not believe in God at all—has grown. Their survey of more than 4,700 US adults found that one-third of Americans say they do not believe in the God of the Bible but that they do believe there is some other higher power or spiritual force in the universe. A slim majority of Americans (56 percent) say they believe in God as described in the Bible. And one in ten do not believe in any higher power or spiritual force. This is a critical factor to consider regarding Christians because the Bible tells us that it is impossible to please God if you don't believe that He is.[33] This is a good segue to the current state of America. Let us take a moment to emphasize how serious the decay of our society has become. According to an article in Prophecy News Watch,[34] there was a time when the following happened:

- Abortionists were sent to prison.
- Pregnancy out of wedlock was thought of as scandalous.
- Homosexuality was considered unnatural and immoral.
- Pornography was despised as a perversion.
- Drugs were something you bought at a drugstore.

- Marriage was sacred.
- Living together was taboo.
- Divorce was a disgrace.
- Same-sex marriage was beyond even the wildest and most depraved imagination.
- Homemaking was honored, and day care was provided by mothers in their homes. Child abuse was almost unheard of.
- Ladies did not curse or smoke.
- The word *damn* was considered flagrant language in a movie.

In America today, none of the above items are viewed this way. America is practicing ungodliness as we kick God out of our schools and all aspects of our public life. America is practicing unrighteousness in the daily murder of babies (Roe v. Wade). America suppresses the truth of the origin of the universe and of life. America is worshiping the creation rather than the creator. America may have signed its death warrant on June 26, 2015, when the Supreme Court rendered its ungodly decision to legalize same-sex marriage. However, America is not alone. Europe has rejected Christianity, and Christians are being persecuted and slaughtered worldwide. Our world is a ticking time bomb. And one of the tragedies is that the average person is just going about his or her normal business as if nothing is wrong, oblivious to the fact that the wrath of God is about to be poured out. No doubt we are witnesses to the very signs that Jesus Christ is soon to return.

The State of Pastors

According to an article in Prophecy News Watch,[35] many pastors seem to have an unwritten eleventh commandment, "Thou shalt not offend." Dr. Michael Brown stated, "I'm aware, of course, that there are megachurches famous for failing to preach against sin. And I'm aware that far too many leaders avoid addressing cultural issues like the plague. And to the extent that these ministries see *success*, this would indicate that there is always a large audience for a nonconfrontational, 'baby food' gospel. It breaks my heart to hear leaders dance around controversial issues. It saddens me deeply when I see people drawn to a message that bypasses the cross and calls for neither sacrifice nor service." Dr. Brown raises a concern that all Christians should be alarmed about. Is your pastor one who is nonconfrontational on addressing cultural issues and providing "baby food" gospel? If so, you may want to carefully decide if you should remain in your church or seek another church that will address the theological impact of political and cultural issues of the day (e.g., racism, classism, homosexuality, social justice system, and other issues you may have questions about).

The traditional roles of pastors are changing. *CBS This Morning*, on September 6, 2018, reported that couples are using friends, family members, and teachers to officiate and perform their weddings (read *Altering Traditions* article). Other pastoral roles to be concerned about are their top five frustrations: (1) many pastors are frustrated with the lack of commitment among laypeople, (2) low level of spiritual maturity among churchgoers, (3) financial and administrative duties, (4) church politics, and (5) implementing change in the church.[36] Three additional frustrations that carry significant weight in ministry were how to do effective outreach, counseling, and developing community within the congregation. The following percentages of pastors rated themselves as excellent in ministry tasks listed below:

- Preaching and teaching: 57 percent
- Knowledge of scripture: 48 percent
- Practical or applied theology: 42 percent
- Leading the organization: 29 percent
- Connecting with surrounding community: 29 percent
- Managing the church's finance: 28 percent
- Counseling or pastoral care: 24 percent
- Prioritizing their own spiritual growth: 22 percent
- Using technology effectively for ministry: 18 percent
- Managing the staff: 16 percent
- Mentoring younger leaders: 14 percent

- Evangelizing people: 10 percent
- Mobilizing volunteers: 6 percent

These pastoral roles or tasks were the result of George Barna's report on the state of pastors. His report assessed how today's faith leaders were navigating life and leadership in an age of complexity. More importantly, with regard to cultural leadership, 85 percent of pastors believe religious freedom is weakening and most believe it's likely that Christian's ability to practice their faith will be restricted in the next decade. For example, looking at the impact of higher Christian education from a cultural leadership perspective, the *Yale Daily News* reported[37] that a large number of Yale University freshmen consider themselves part of the LGBTQ community than those who self-identify as conservatives. More than half of all first-year students took part in a survey that gauged their opinions, interests, and goals, according to the *Yale Daily News*. Of the 864 respondents, just 9 percent said they viewed themselves as *somewhat conservative* while 1 percent said they were *very conservative*. As for LGBTQ students, nearly 5 percent (of respondents) identify as gay and just over 9 percent as bisexual or transsexual. There were 3 percent who opted not to answer, and the remaining 8 percent identified as asexual, ace spectrum, or questioning their sexual orientation. Those who can be categorized in the LGBTQ grouping even outnumbered prominent religious sects. Combined, there are more LGBTQ freshmen at Yale than there are Protestant students (16 percent) or Catholics (15 percent). In May, a Gallup poll showed that 4.5 percent of Americans identified as LGBTQ in 2017. Yale's formal slogan is "Lux et veritas" or "Light and Truth." God isn't very welcome at Yale these days despite its prestigious (and very religious) origins, but most interesting is the fact that LGBTQ people are wildly over-represented at Yale. Less than 5 percent of Americans identify as LGBTQ, but a combined 14 percent of Yale students do. Imagine what impact Yale University will have on its future leaders from a cultural leadership standpoint. Imagine the impact on future cultural leadership if other universities are experiencing what Yale is experiencing.

Another unfortunate factor of great concern today is sexual abuse by clergy. *World* magazine reported this is not only a problem in the Catholic church but is also a problem in Protestant churches.[38] The article references three church environments in which clergy are most vulnerable: (1) congregations that have dominating pastors with unchecked authority; (2) conference and lecture circuits with celebrities and quasi celebrities who come to cities for weekend workshops and one-night lectures that provide opportunities to sin and go, leaving behind casualties; and (3) megachurch leaders facing extraordinary pressure to cover up problems, knowing the risks of media exposure.

Staying the Course According to God's Promises

From our physical birth to our physical death is our probationary period for God to determine whether we should be given a permanent place in His kingdom and receive rewards. Unless we experience a spiritual birth during our life's journey, we will not secure a permanent place in the Kingdom of God. God's will for our lives requires us to be in the right place at the right time, doing the right things, which is why He set boundaries in His Word.[39] Every act of God in our lives is designed to increase our dependence upon Him. Every assignment He gives us will require His participation to succeed. God directs the steps of those who stand on His promises.[40] God has blessed us with every spiritual blessing in the heavenly places in Christ.[41]

Staying the course means examining the direction of Christian Education and how Christian Colleges and Universities prepare for the future. Barna's study on this subject,[42] in partnership with the Association for Biblical Higher Education, revealed 14 percent of all US adults and self-identified Christians eighteen and older expressed they believed the purpose of going to college was to develop moral character. Only 7 percent of all US adults and self-identified Christians eighteen and older expressed they believed the purpose of going to college was to encourage spiritual growth. However, 70 percent of those surveyed rated preparation for a specific job or career as the primary purpose for going to college. Clearly the percentages show that developing moral character and spiritual growth did not rate high as purposes for going to college. This supports the moral decline in American society. Other relevant factors, such as historical orthodox beliefs about human sexuality, may place increasing risks of Christian institutions running afoul of the law and losing eligibility to accept federal or state financial aid. Society's moral compass is shifting away from the authority of scripture to self or human authority; not to mention the economic pressures on families with the rising costs of education.

Staying the course means standing firm on the Word of God and not on political, social, or peer pressure. Staying the course means calling what God says is sin and not an addiction, mental or medical condition, pro-choice, or alternative lifestyle. When we engage the subject of abortion, homosexuality, and same-sex marriage, we should love the sinner but hate the sin. We must love and respect abortionists and homosexuals. We must not demonize them because of their sinful behavior or any other person's sinful behavior. We must model the attitudes or behaviors God commands of us. Blessed are those who do His commandments.

Staying the course means understanding that the world is experiencing sorrows as described in Matthew 24.[43] We must keep God's Word in our hearts and pray without ceasing, looking above for our hope and promise. Whoever listens to God will dwell safely and be secure without fear of evil.[44] We must stand firm against persecution and compromise. It's later than we think with regard to the end of the age. Christ's return is imminent to deliver those who are righteous and judge those who are wicked.

We cannot stand on God's promises if we don't believe in Him. We cannot stand on God's promises if we have not heard Him. If we don't hear Him, we will lack faith. Our faith comes by hearing and hearing by the Word of God. How can we hear without a preacher who God sends? How beautiful are the feet of those who preach the gospel of peace, who bring glad tidings of good things? Now more than ever, believers on the Lord Jesus Christ must stay the course. To do that, we must have a clear understanding of why God created us and His mission and vision for our lives. God created us to serve Him using the gifts and talents He placed in us.[45] His mission for us is to seek His kingdom first and His righteousness; go and make disciples of all nations baptizing them in the name of the Father, Son, and Holy Spirit.[46] God's vision for us is to teach those who believe on Him everything He has commanded us so He can pour out His Spirit on everyone who calls upon His name.[47] He will be with us to the end of the age. Hallelujah!

Let me close with the lyrics of the hymn "Standing on the Promises":

Standing on the promises of Christ my King
Through eternal ages let his praises ring
Glory in the highest I will shout and sing
Standing on the promises of God

Standing, standing
Standing on the promises of God my Savior
Standing, standing
I'm standing on the promises of God

Standing on the promises, I cannot fall
Listening every moment to the Spirit's call
Resting in my Savior as my all in all
Standing on the promises of God

Standing, standing
Standing on the promises of Christ my Savior
Standing, standing
I'm standing on the promises of God

Endnotes

1.   "For to us a child is born, to us a son is given, and the government will be on His shoulders. And He will be called Wonderful Counselor, Mighty God, Everlasting Father, Prince of Peace. Of the greatness of His government and peace there will be no end. He will reign on David's throne and over his kingdom, establishing and upholding it with justice and righteousness from that time on and forever. The zeal of the Lord Almighty will accomplish this" (Isaiah 9:6–7).

2.   "For the Lord God is a sun and shield; the Lord bestows favor and honor; no good thing does He withhold from those whose walk is blameless" (Psalm 84:11).

3.   "Now it shall come to pass, if you diligently obey the voice of the Lord your God, to observe carefully all His commandments which I command you today, that the Lord your God will set you high above all nations of the earth. And all these blessings shall come upon you and overtake you because you obey the voice of the Lord your God. You will be blessed in the city and blessed in the country.

   The fruit of your womb will be blessed, and the crops of your land and the young of your livestock—the calves of your herds and the lambs of your flocks.

   Your basket and your kneading trough will be blessed.

   You will be blessed when you come in and blessed when you go out.

   The Lord will grant that the enemies who rise up against you will be defeated before you. They will come at you from one direction but flee from you in seven.

   The Lord will send a blessing on your barns and on everything you put your hand to. The Lord your God will bless you in the land He is giving you.

   The Lord will establish you as His holy people, as He promised you an oath if you keep the commands of the Lord your God and walk in obedience to Him. Then all the peoples on earth will see that you are called by the name of the Lord, and they will fear you. The Lord will grant you abundant prosperity—in the fruit of your womb, the young of your livestock, and the crops of your ground—in the land He swore to your ancestors to give you.

   The Lord will open the heavens, the storehouse of His bounty, to send rain on your land in season and to bless all the work of your hands. You will lend to many nations but will borrow from none.

The Lord will make you the head, not the tail. If you pay attention to the commands of the Lord your God that I give you this day and carefully follow them, you will always be at the top, never at the bottom. Do not turn aside from any of the commands I give you today, to the right or to the left, following other gods and serving them.

Curses for Disobedience

However, if you do not obey the Lord your God and do not carefully follow all His commands and decrees, I am giving you today, all these curses will come on you and overtake you:

You will be cursed in the city and cursed in the country.

Your basket and your kneading trough will be cursed.

The fruit of your womb will be cursed, and the crops of your land, and the calves of your herds, and the lambs of your flocks.

You will be cursed when you come in and cursed when you go out.

The Lord will send on you curses, confusion, and rebuke in everything you put your hand to, until you are destroyed and come to sudden ruin because of the evil you have done in forsaking Him.

The Lord will plague you with diseases until He has destroyed you from the land you are entering to possess.

The Lord will strike you with wasting disease, with fever and inflammation, with scorching heat and drought, with blight and mildew, which will plague you until you perish.

The sky over your head will be bronze, the ground beneath you iron.

The Lord will turn the rain of your country into dust and powder; it will come down from the skies until you are destroyed.

The Lord will cause you to be defeated before your enemies. You will come at them from one direction but flee from them in seven, and you will become a thing of horror to all the kingdoms on earth.

Your carcasses will be food for all the birds and the wild animals, and there will be no one to frighten them away.

The Lord will afflict you with the boils of Egypt and with tumors, festering sores, and the itch, from which you cannot be cured.

The Lord will afflict you with madness, blindness, and confusion of mind.

At midday you will grope about like a blind person in the dark. You will be unsuccessful in everything you do; day after day you will be oppressed and robbed, with no one to rescue you." (Deuteronomy 28:1–29).

[4] George Barna, "Articles in Culture and Media," December 27, 2017, https://www.barna.com/research/year-review-barnas-10-read-articles-2017. He founded the Barna Research Group in 1984 (now The Barna Group) and helped it become a leading marketing research firm focused on the intersection of faith and culture before selling it in 2009. Through the Barna Group, George has served several hundred parachurch ministries, thousands of Christian

churches, and many other nonprofit and for-profit organizations as well as the US military. He currently serves as the executive director of the American Culture and Faith Institute (a division of United in Purpose) and is President of Metaformation (a faith development organization). Barna has written more than fifty books, mostly addressing cultural trends, leadership, spiritual development, and church dynamics. They include New York Times best sellers and several award-winning books. He has sold more books based on survey research related to matters of faith than any author in American history. His work is frequently cited as an authoritative source by the media. Barna has been hailed as the most quoted person in the Christian church today and has been named by various media as one of the nation's most influential Christian leaders.

5   The American Culture and Faith Institute (ACFI), a division of United in Purpose—Education, is a nonpartisan, not-for-profit research organization that regularly conducts national surveys to gauge the sentiment and activity of politically conservative and spiritually active Christians in America. The information gained from these studies is used in various ways: to help UiP in its planning and outreach efforts, to support UiP's organizational partners in their efforts to impact their circles of influence, to educate the public by sharing insights about conservatives through the media, and to educate Christian church leaders about the people they serve.

6   "Introduction to the Sermon on the Mount
     Now when Jesus saw the crowds, He went up on a mountainside and sat down. His disciples came to Him, and He began to teach them.

The Beatitudes

He said:
'Blessed are the poor in spirit, for theirs is the kingdom of heaven. Blessed are those who mourn, for they will be comforted. Blessed are the meek, for they will inherit the earth. Blessed are those who hunger and thirst for righteousness, for they will be filled.

Blessed are the merciful, for they will be shown mercy. Blessed are the pure in heart, for they will see God. Blessed are the peacemakers, for they will be called children of God. Blessed are those who are persecuted because of righteousness, for theirs is the kingdom of heaven. Blessed are you when people insult you, persecute you, and falsely say all kinds of evil against you because of me. Rejoice and be glad because great is your reward in heaven, for in the same way they persecuted the prophets who were before you.'

Salt and Light

You are the salt of the earth. But if the salt loses its saltiness, how can it be made salty again? It is no longer good for anything, except to be thrown out and trampled underfoot.

You are the light of the world. A town built on a hill cannot be hidden. Neither do people light a lamp and put it under a bowl. Instead they put it on its stand, and it gives light to everyone in the house. In the same way, let your light shine before others, that they may see your good deeds and glorify your Father in heaven.

The Fulfillment of the Law

Do not think that I have come to abolish the Law or the Prophets; I have not come to abolish them but to fulfill them. For truly I tell you, until heaven and earth disappear, not the smallest letter, not the least stroke of a pen, will by any means disappear from the Law until everything is accomplished. Therefore anyone who sets aside one of the least of these commands and teaches others accordingly will be called least in the kingdom of heaven, but whoever practices and teaches these commands will be called great in the kingdom of heaven. For I tell you that unless your righteousness surpasses that of the Pharisees and the teachers of the law, you will certainly not enter the kingdom of heaven.

Murder

You have heard that it was said to the people long ago, 'You shall not murder, and anyone who murders will be subject to judgment.' But I tell you that anyone who is angry with a brother or sister will be subject to judgment. Again, anyone who says to a brother or sister, 'Raca,' is answerable to the court. And anyone who says, 'You fool!' will be in danger of the fire of hell.

Therefore, if you are offering your gift at the altar and there remember that your brother or sister has something against you, leave your gift there in front of the altar. First go and be reconciled to them; then come and offer your gift.

Settle matters quickly with your adversary who is taking you to court. Do it while you are still together on the way, or your adversary may hand you over to the judge, and the judge may hand you over to the officer, and you may be thrown into prison. Truly I tell you, you will not get out until you have paid the last penny.

Adultery

You have heard that it was said, 'You shall not commit adultery.' But I tell you that anyone who looks at a woman lustfully has already committed adultery with her in his heart. If your right eye causes you to stumble, gouge it out and throw it away. It is better for you to lose one part of your body than for your whole body to be thrown into hell. And if your right hand causes you to stumble, cut it off and throw it away. It is better for you to lose one part of your body than for your whole body to go into hell.

Divorce

It has been said, 'Anyone who divorces his wife must give her a certificate of divorce.' But I tell you that anyone who divorces his wife, except for sexual immorality, makes her the victim of adultery, and anyone who marries a divorced woman commits adultery.

Oaths

Again, you have heard that it was said to the people long ago, 'Do not break your oath, but fulfill to the Lord the vows you have made.' But I tell you, do not swear an oath at all: either by heaven, for it is God's throne; or by the earth, for it is His footstool; or by Jerusalem, for it is the city of the Great King. And do not swear by your head, for you cannot make even one hair white or black. All you need to say is simply 'Yes' or 'No'; anything beyond this comes from the evil one.

Eye for Eye

You have heard that it was said, 'Eye for eye, and tooth for tooth.' But I tell you, do not resist an evil person. If anyone slaps you on the right cheek, turn to them the other cheek also. And if anyone wants to sue you and take your shirt, hand over your coat as well. If anyone forces you to go one mile, go with them two miles. Give to the one who asks you, and do not turn away from the one who wants to borrow from you.

Love for Enemies

You have heard that it was said, 'Love your neighbor and hate your enemy.' But I tell you, love your enemies and pray for those who persecute you, that you may be children of your Father in heaven. He causes His sun to rise on the evil and the good, and sends rain on the righteous and the unrighteous. If you love those who love you, what reward will you get? Are not even the tax collectors doing that? And if you greet only your own people, what are you doing more than others? Do not even pagans do that? Be perfect, therefore, as your heavenly Father is perfect.

Giving to the Needy

Be careful not to practice your righteousness in front of others to be seen by them. If you do, you will have no reward from your Father in heaven.

So when you give to the needy, do not announce it with trumpets, as the hypocrites do in the synagogues and on the streets, to be honored by others. Truly I tell you, they have received their reward in full. But when you give to the needy, do not let your left hand know what your right hand is doing so that your giving may be in secret. Then your Father, who sees what is done in secret, will reward you.

Prayer

And when you pray, do not be like the hypocrites, for they love to pray standing in the synagogues and on the street corners to be seen by others. Truly I tell you, they have received their reward in full. But when you pray, go into your room, close the door, and pray to your Father, who is unseen. Then your Father, who sees what is done in secret, will reward you. And when you pray, do not keep on babbling like pagans, for they think they will be heard because of their many words. Do not be like them, for your Father knows what you need before you ask Him.

This, then, is how you should pray: 'Our Father in heaven, hallowed be your name,

Your kingdom come, your will be done, on earth as it is in heaven. Give us today our daily bread. And forgive us our debts, as we also have forgiven our debtors.

And lead us not into temptation but deliver us from the evil one.' For if you forgive other people when they sin against you, your heavenly Father will also forgive you. But if you do not forgive others their sins, your Father will not forgive your sins.

Fasting

When you fast, do not look somber as the hypocrites do, for they disfigure their faces to show others they are fasting. Truly I tell you, they have received their reward in full. But when you fast, put oil on your head and wash your face so that it will not be obvious to others that you are fasting but only to your Father, who is unseen; and your Father, who sees what is done in secret, will reward you.

Treasures in Heaven

Do not store up for yourselves treasures on earth, where moths and vermin destroy, and where thieves break in and steal. But store up for yourselves treasures in heaven, where moths and vermin do not destroy, and where thieves do not break in and steal. For where your treasure is, there your heart will be also.

The eye is the lamp of the body. If your eyes are healthy, your whole body will be full of light. But if your eyes are unhealthy, your whole body will be full of darkness. If then the light within you is darkness, how great is that darkness!

No one can serve two masters. Either you will hate the one and love the other, or you will be devoted to the one and despise the other. You cannot serve both God and money.

Do Not Worry

Therefore I tell you, do not worry about your life, what you will eat or drink; or about your body, what you will wear. Is not life more than food, and the body more than clothes? Look at the birds of the air; they do not sow or reap or store away in barns, and yet your heavenly Father feeds them. Are you not much more valuable than they? Can anyone of you, by worrying, add a single hour to your life?

And why do you worry about clothes? See how the flowers of the field grow. They do not labor or spin. Yet I tell you that not even Solomon in all his splendor was dressed like one of these. If that is how God clothes the grass of the field, which is here today and tomorrow is thrown into the fire, will He not much more clothe you—you of little faith? So do not worry, saying, 'What shall we eat?' or 'What shall we drink?' or 'What shall we wear?' For the pagans run after all these things, and your heavenly Father knows that you need them. But seek first His kingdom and His righteousness, and all these things will be given to you as well. Therefore do not worry about tomorrow, for tomorrow will worry about itself. Each day has enough trouble of its own.

Judging Others

Do not judge, or you, too, will be judged. For in the same way you judge others, you will be judged, and with the measure you use, it will be measured to you.

Why do you look at the speck of sawdust in your brother's eye and pay no attention to the plank in your own eye? How can you say to your brother, 'Let me take the speck out of your eye,' when all the time there is a plank in your own eye? You hypocrite, first take the plank out of your own eye, and then you will see clearly to remove the speck from your brother's eye.

Do not give dogs what is sacred; do not throw your pearls to pigs. If you do, they may trample them under their feet and turn and tear you to pieces.

Ask, Seek, Knock

Ask and it will be given to you; seek and you will find; knock and the door will be opened to you. For everyone who asks receives; the one who seeks finds; and to the one who knocks, the door will be opened.

Which of you, if your son asks for bread, will give him a stone? Or if he asks for a fish, will give him a snake? If you, then, though you are evil, know how to give good gifts to your children, how much more will your Father in heaven give good gifts to those who ask Him! So in everything, do to others what you would have them do to you, for this sums up the Law and the Prophets.

The Narrow and Wide Gates

Enter through the narrow gate. For wide is the gate and broad is the road that leads to destruction, and many enter through it. But small is the gate and narrow the road that leads to life, and only a few find it.

True and False Prophets

Watch out for false prophets. They come to you in sheep's clothing, but inwardly they are ferocious wolves. By their fruit you will recognize them. Do people pick grapes from thorn bushes or figs from thistles? Likewise, every good tree bears good fruit, but a bad tree bears bad fruit. A good tree cannot bear bad fruit, and a bad tree cannot bear good fruit. Every tree that does not bear good fruit is cut down and thrown into the fire. Thus, by their fruit, you will recognize them.

True and False Disciples

Not everyone who says to me, 'Lord, Lord,' will enter the kingdom of heaven, but only the one who does the will of my Father who is in heaven. Many will say to me on that day, 'Lord, Lord, did we not prophesy in your name and in your name drive out demons, and in your name perform many miracles?' Then I will tell them plainly, 'I never knew you. Away from me, you evildoers!'

The Wise and Foolish Builders

Therefore everyone who hears these words of mine and puts them into practice is like a wise man who built his house on the rock. The rain came down, the streams rose, and the winds blew and beat against that house; yet it did not fall because it had its foundation on the rock. But everyone who hears these words of mine and does not put them into practice is like a foolish man who built his house on sand. The rain came down, the streams rose, and the winds blew and beat against that house, and it fell with a great crash.

When Jesus had finished saying these things, the crowds were amazed at His teaching because He taught as one who had authority and not as their teachers of the law" (Beatitudes, Matthew 5–7).

7   Barna defined this as deinstitutionalization and individualism which has, for many, moved spiritual practice away from the public rituals of institutional Christianity to the private experience of God within.

8   Barna defined this as those who consider themselves "spiritual" but say their religious faith is not very important in their life; though some may self-identify as members of a religious faith.

9   "Dear friend, I pray that you may enjoy good health and that all may go well with you, even as your soul is getting along well" (3 John 2).

10   "The thief comes only to steal and kill and destroy; I have come that they may have life and have it to the full" (John 10:10).

11   "Love is patient; love is kind. It does not envy; it does not boast; it is not proud" (1 Corinthians 13:4).

12   "Then God said, 'Let us make mankind in our image, in our likeness, so that they may rule over the fish in the sea and the birds in the sky, over the livestock and all the wild animals, and over all the creatures that move along the ground.' So God created mankind in His own image, in the image of God, He created them; male and female, He created them" (Genesis 1:26–27).

13   "They came to Capernaum. When He was in the house, He asked them, 'What were you arguing about on the road?' But they kept quiet because on the way they had argued about who was the greatest. Sitting down, Jesus called the twelve and said, 'Anyone who wants to be first must be the very last and the servant of all'" (Mark 9:33–35)

14   "The Lord had said to Abram, 'Go from your country, your people, and your father's household to the land I will show you. I will make you into a great nation, and I will bless you; I will make your name great, and you will be a

blessing. I will bless those who bless you, and whoever curses you I will curse; and all peoples on earth will be blessed through you" (Genesis 12:1–3).

15 "He redeemed us in order that the blessing given to Abraham might come to the Gentiles through Christ Jesus so that by faith we might receive the promise of the Spirit. The promises were spoken to Abraham and to his seed. Scripture does not say "and to seeds," meaning many people, but "and to your seed," meaning one person, who is Christ" (Galatians 3:14 and 3:16).

16 "Understand, then, that those who have faith are children of Abraham. Scripture foresaw that God would justify the Gentiles by faith and announced the gospel in advance to Abraham: 'All nations will be blessed through you.' So those who rely on faith are blessed along with Abraham, the man of faith" (Galatians 3:7–9).

17 "So those who rely on faith are blessed along with Abraham, the man of faith" (Galatians 3:9).

18 "If you belong to Christ, then you are Abraham's seed and heirs according to the promise" (Galatians 3:29).

19 "If you declare with your mouth, 'Jesus is Lord,' and believe in your heart that God raised Him from the dead, you will be saved. For it is with your heart that you believe and are justified, and it is with your mouth that you profess your faith and are saved. As scripture says, 'Anyone who believes in Him will never be put to shame.' For there is no difference between Jew and Gentile—the same Lord is Lord of all and richly blesses all who call on Him, for 'Everyone who calls on the name of the Lord will be saved'" (Romans 10:9–13).

20 "The Lord will fight for me; I need only be still" (Exodus 14:14).

21 "He gives strength to the weary and increases the power of the weak. Even youths grow tired and weary, and young men stumble and fall; but those who hope in the Lord will renew their strength. They will soar on wings like eagles; they will run and not grow weary, they will walk and not be faint" (Isaiah 40:29–31).

22 "'Though the mountains be shaken, and the hills be removed, yet my unfailing love for you will not be shaken nor my covenant of peace be removed,' says the Lord, who has compassion on you" (Isaiah 54:10).

23 "So do not fear, for I am with you; do not be dismayed, for I am your God. I will strengthen you and help you; I will uphold you with my righteous right hand" (Isaiah 41:10).

24 "If any of you lacks wisdom, you should ask God, who gives generously to all without finding fault, and it will be given to you" (James 1:5).

25 "If we confess our sins, He is faithful and just and will forgive us our sins and purify us from all unrighteousness" (1 John 1:9).

26 "Whoever acknowledges me before others, I will also acknowledge before my Father in heaven" (Matthew 10:32).

27 "But remember the Lord your God, for it is He who gives you the ability to produce wealth, and so confirms His covenant, which He swore to your ancestors,

as it is today. The blessing of the Lord brings wealth, without painful toil for it" (Deuteronomy 8:18 and Proverbs 10:22).

28 "Then you will understand the fear of the Lord and find the knowledge of God. For the Lord gives wisdom; from His mouth come knowledge and understanding. He holds success in store for the upright; He is a shield to those whose walk is blameless, for He guards the course of the just and protects the way of His faithful ones. Then you will understand what is right and just and fair—every good path. For wisdom will enter your heart, and knowledge will be pleasant to your soul.

Discretion will protect you, and understanding will guard you. Wisdom will save you from the ways of wicked men, from men whose words are perverse, who have left the straight paths to walk in dark ways" (Proverbs 2:5–13).

29 The Christian Journal reported Reverend Yolanda Norton said the mass was about "naming black female spirituality" as it's embodied in Beyoncé's songs. Using the song "Flaws and All," Norton quotes the lyrics, "I'm a train wreck in the morning, I'm a b—— in the afternoon, every now and then without warning, I can be really mean toward you." She explains that Grace Church is using this song as a prayer to God during worship. At Coachella, Beyoncé performed as the Egyptian queen Nefertiti. And at the Fifty-Ninth Grammy Awards, Beyoncé presented herself as a mother goddess that according to Harper's Bazaar, "invoked multiracial goddesses—from the Yoruba Orisha Oshun to Hindi goddess Kali to the Catholic Black Madonna—and heralded the divine beauty and aura of black motherhood." The Beyoncé Mass was part of a three-part series at Grace Church, San Francisco, California, that started with a program on Mary Magdalene called The Original Nasty Woman. While feminism in the form of worshiping "divine black motherhood" is on the rise, the Bible makes it clear that we should love the Lord our God and serve only Him. Psalm 106:36 tells us that in the past, when people served their idols, they became a snare to them ("Beyoncé's Family Buys a Church, Goddess Worship May Have Just Gone to a Whole New Level," Christian Journal).

30 George Barna, "Articles in Culture and Media," December 27, 2017, https://www.barna.com/research/year-review-barnas-10-read-articles-2017. He founded the Barna Research Group in 1984 (now The Barna Group) and helped it become a leading marketing research firm focused on the intersection of faith and culture before selling it in 2009. Through the Barna Group, George has served several hundred parachurch ministries, thousands of Christian churches, and many other nonprofit and for-profit organizations as well as the US military. He currently serves as the executive director of the American Culture and Faith Institute (a division of United in Purpose) and is President of Metaformation (a faith development organization). Barna has written more than fifty books, mostly addressing cultural trends, leadership, spiritual development, and church dynamics. They include New York Times best sellers and several award-winning books. He has sold more books based on survey research

related to matters of faith than any author in American history. His work is frequently cited as an authoritative source by the media. Barna has been hailed as the most quoted person in the Christian church today and has been named by various media as one of the nation's most influential Christian leaders.

31 The American Culture and Faith Institute (ACFI), a division of United in Purpose—Education, is a nonpartisan, not-for-profit research organization that regularly conducts national surveys to gauge the sentiment and activity of politically conservative and spiritually active Christians in America. The information gained from these studies is used in various ways: to help UiP in its planning and outreach efforts, to support UiP's organizational partners in their efforts to impact their circles of influence, to educate the public by sharing insights about conservatives through the media, and to educate Christian church leaders about the people they serve.

32 Pew Research Center is a nonpartisan fact tank that informs the public about the issues, attitudes and trends shaping the world. It conducts public opinion polling, demographic research, media content analysis, and other empirical social science research. Pew Research Center does not take policy positions. It is a subsidiary of The Pew Charitable Trusts. "When Americans Say They Believe in God, What Do They Mean," Pew Research Center, April 25, 2018.

33 "And without faith it is impossible to please God because anyone who comes to Him must believe that He exists and that He rewards those who earnestly seek Him" (Hebrews 11:6).

34 David Lamb, "What Is America's Prophetic Destiny? America in Bible Prophecy," Prophecy News Watch, September 11, 2018, http://prophecynewswatch.com.

35 Dr. Michael Brown (www.askdrbrown.org) is the host of the nationally syndicated Line of Fire radio program. His latest book is Playing with Holy Fire: A Wake-Up Call to the Pentecostal-Charismatic Church. Michael L. Brown, August 14, 2018, AskDrBrown.org.

36 George Barna and Pepperdine University, "The State of Pastors."

37 Prophecy News Watch, September 17, 2018.

38 Marvin Olasky, Sophia Lee, and Emily Belz, "Crouching at Every Door," World, September 15, 2018.

39 "From one man, He made all the nations, that they should inhabit the whole earth; and He marked out their appointed times in history and the boundaries of their lands. God did this so that they would seek Him and perhaps reach out for Him and find Him, though He is not far from any one of us" (Acts 17:26–27).

40 "The Lord makes firm the steps of the one who delights in Him; though he may stumble, he will not fall, for the Lord upholds him with His hand" (Psalm 37:23–24).

41 "Praise be to the God and Father of our Lord Jesus Christ, who has blessed us in the heavenly realms with every spiritual blessing in Christ. For He chose us in

Him before the creation of the world to be holy and blameless in His sight. In love He predestined us for adoption to sonship through Jesus Christ, in accordance with His pleasure and will—to the praise of His glorious grace, which He has freely given us in the one He loves" (Ephesians 1:3–6).

42 "What's Next for Christian Higher Education, How Christian Colleges and Universities Can Prepare for the Future."

43 "Jesus answered: 'Watch out that no one deceives you. For many will come in my name, claiming, "I am the Messiah," and will deceive many. You will hear of wars and rumors of wars, but see to it that you are not alarmed. Such things must happen, but the end is still to come. Nation will rise against nation and kingdom against kingdom. There will be famines and earthquakes in various places. All these are the beginning of birth pains. Then you will be handed over to be persecuted and put to death, and you will be hated by all nations because of me. At that time, many will turn away from the faith and will betray and hate each other, and many false prophets will appear and deceive many people. Because of the increase of wickedness, the love of most will grow cold, but the one who stands firm to the end will be saved. And this gospel of the kingdom will be preached in the whole world as a testimony to all nations, and then the end will come'" (Matthew 24:4–14).

44 "But whoever listens to me will live in safety and be at ease, without fear of harm" (Proverbs 1:33).

45 "Offer hospitality to one another without grumbling. Each one should use whatever gift he has received to serve others, faithfully administering God's grace in its various forms" (1 Peter 4:9–10).

46 "Therefore, go and make disciples of all nations, baptizing them in the name of the Father and of the Son and of the Holy Spirit, and teaching them to obey everything I have commanded you. And surely, I am with you always, to the very end of the age" (Matthew 28:19–20).

47 "And afterward, I will pour out my Spirit on all people. Your sons and daughters will prophesy, your old men will dream dreams, your young men will see visions" (Joel 2:28).

About the Authors

 M. Lamont Rucker is a native of Washington, DC. He matriculated in the DC public school system, graduating from Eastern Senior High School in Northeast Washington, DC. He is married to his lovely wife, Pamela, who is also a native of Washington, DC, and graduate of Eastern Senior High School. They are a blended family with three daughters—Latasha, Michelle, and Tiffany—and a son, Charles. They all reside in the DC Metropolitan area.

Mr. Rucker retired in 2002 after serving thirty years with the federal government. He served as Human Capital Officer with the US Mint Philadelphia; Director of Labor Relations with the US Mint Headquarters Washington, DC; and several other human resource management positions with the Department of Commerce, Department of Housing and Urban Development, and US Treasury's Bureau of the Public Debt. Since his retirement, he served as an Employee Labor Relations Consultant with the Department of Homeland Security.

Pamela Rucker served in several human resources management positions with Department of the Treasury's Comptroller of the Currency and the Office of Financial Stability (Obama TARP Initiative); Department of Justice's Alcohol Tobacco, Firearms, and Explosives; Department of Homeland Security's Immigration and Customs Enforcement; and Customs and Border Protection, where she served as the Chief of Workforce Planning and Development. She presently serves as a Management and Program Analyst.

In 1993, Mr. Rucker was called to preach the gospel of the Lord Jesus Christ. From 1993, he served in the African Methodist Episcopal Zion Church, Philadelphia–Baltimore Episcopal District as an Associate Minister and Christian Education Director. In 1999, he was appointed as senior pastor of Alleyne Memorial AME Zion Church in Philadelphia, Pennsylvania. In 2005, the Lord led him to plant Truth Temple Bible Church in Waldorf, Maryland. In 2008, Mr. Rucker transitioned from the pastoral ministry and served as a premarital or couples' counselor. Mr. Rucker holds an associate of arts degree in biblical studies, a bachelor of science degree in Bible, a master of divinity degree, and an honorary doctor of divinity degree. Mrs. Rucker attended the University of the District of Columbia, majoring in public speaking. She earned Ministry Internship I and II certifications from Spirit of Faith Christian Center. Presently, Mr. Rucker and his wife, Pamela, are members of the First Baptist Church of Glenarden in Upper Marlboro, Maryland. John K. Jenkins Sr. is the senior pastor.

CPSIA information can be obtained
at www.ICGtesting.com
Printed in the USA
BVHW032357120919
558329BV00006B/49/P

9 781684 561285